SRI LANKA TRAVEL GUIDE

Sri Lanka Travel Guide: Explore Local Culture and Essential Tips for an Unforgettable Journey

Michael Keenan

All rights reserved. No part of this publication may be reproduced, distributed, or transmitted in any form or by any means, including photocopying, recording, or other electronic or mechanical methods, without the prior written permission of the publisher, except in the case of brief quotations embodied in critical reviews and certain other non-commercial uses permitted by copyright law.

Copyright © Michael Keenan.

My Vacation Trip to Sri Lanka: A Journey of Discovery and Adventure..................................3
Sri Lanka Population.. 8

Chapter 1: Sri Lanka ,The True Gem of the world... 9
What Makes Sri Lanka a Famous Tourist Paradise... 10
Who would benefit from visiting Sri Lanka?... 12
Desirable Locations for first time visitors in Sri Lanka... 13

Chapter 2: Planning a Journey to Sri Lanka... 15
What is the optimal period for traveling to Sri Lanka... 16
Month by Month Weather in Sri Lanka.......17
How to Journey to Sri Lanka......................... 22
Air Travel to Sri Lanka: Expenses and Costs..

22

Road Travel to Sri Lanka and its Expenses. 24

Traveling to Sri Lanka by Sea: Process and Costs..25

Prominent Tourist Destinations for Accommodation in Sri Lanka.......................27

Essential Packing Guide for Your Journey to Sri Lanka...29

Crafting Your Ideal Itinerary: How Long to Stay in Sri Lanka..32

Chapter 3: Understanding Sri Lanka Entry 34

Requirements: A Comprehensive Guide......34

Visa Types for Sri Lanka visitors..................34

Proof of Accommodation in Sri Lanka.........36

Proof of Financial Capability for Traveling to Sri Lanka...38

Chapter 4: Lodging Choices and Expenses in Sri Lanka...40

Hotel Bookings and Tips in Sri Lanka..........42

Luxury Hotels in Sri Lanka...........................45

Cheap and affordable Hotels in Sri Lanka.. 48

Romantic hotels in Sri Lanka........................51

Camping and Glamping in Sri Lanka by Tourists.. 55

Chapter 5: Nightlife and Dining Etiquette in Sri Lanka..57
Sri Lanka Nightlife... 58
Must Try Sri Lanka Food And Cuisines...... 60
Sri Lanka Famous Drinks..............................63
Best Cafes and Restaurants in Sri Lanka.....66
Sri Lanka Dining Etiquette............................69

Chapter 6: Top Attractions in Sri Lanka And Fun Activities For First Time Visitors...........72
Sri Lanka landmarks.......................................72
Sri Lanka beaches...74
Enchanting Gardens in Sri Lanka................ 77
Sri Lanka Museums And Educational Attraction... 78
Zoos and Animal Encounters in Sri Lanka..81

Chapter 7: Transit Options And Costs For Getting Around In Sri Lanka........................84
Sri Lanka Bus Service.................................... 84
Car rental in Sri Lanka..................................86

Train Services in Sri Lanka............................ 88
Sri Lanka Ferry Transit System..................... 91

Chapter 8: The "Must know" Guidelines For First-time Visitors To Sri Lanka................... 94
Sri Lanka Currency... 94
Bring some Cash with you for Sri Lanka Tour 95
Where To Exchange Money in Sri Lanka.... 97
Health Tips for Sri Lanka Tourists................ 99
Sri Lanka Emergency Contacts.................... 101
Sri Lanka Cultural Étiquettes...................... 102

Chapter 9: Financial Planning and Budgeting for Sri Lanka tour.. 104
The Need For Financial Planning As A Tourist in Sri Lanka....................................... 105
Money Saving For First Time Tourists to Sri Lanka.. 108
Tips for Bargaining and Negotiating in Sri Lanka.. 110
Tips To help Avoid Crowds While Shopping/ Touring Sri Lanka... 112

5

Chapter 10: Sri Lanka Day Trips & Excursions..114
Nature and Wildlife in Sri Lanka.................114
Sri Lanka Solo Travel...................................117
Safety Tips for Sri Lanka Solo travelers.... 119
7-Day Sri Lanka Travel Plan......................121
Helpful websites and Resources for Tourists in Sri Lanka...124
Tourists friendly Apps.................................125
Conclusion..126

My Vacation Trip to Sri Lanka: A Journey of Discovery and Adventure

My vacation trip to Sri Lanka was a journey that exceeded every expectation, filled with discovery, adventure, and profound cultural encounters. Landing in Colombo, the bustling capital, I was immediately swept up in its vibrant energy. Exploring the Pettah Market, I was immersed in a sensory overload of spices, textiles, and the friendly banter of local vendors.

Venturing further, I delved into Colombo's colonial past, marveling at the grandeur of the Independence Memorial Hall and the historic charm of Galle Face Green. The juxtaposition of modern skyscrapers against colonial architecture painted a vivid picture of the city's evolution.

Leaving Colombo behind, I embarked on a journey through Sri Lanka's ancient history.

Anuradhapura, the ancient capital, was a mesmerizing experience. Standing before the towering stupas of Ruwanwelisaya and Jetavanaramaya, I felt a deep sense of reverence and awe. The sacred Bodhi Tree, said to be a descendant of the original tree under which Buddha attained enlightenment, exuded an aura of tranquility.

Next, Polonnaruwa transported me back in time with its well-preserved ruins and intricately carved statues of Buddha. Cycling through the ancient city, I marveled at the engineering prowess of the Parakrama Samudra, a vast reservoir that still irrigates the surrounding lands.

The journey into Sri Lanka's hill country was a scenic marvel. Nuwara Eliya, with its cool climate and verdant tea plantations, offered a serene escape. Wandering through rows of neatly trimmed tea bushes, I learned about the art of tea plucking and savored a freshly brewed cup overlooking mist-shrouded mountains.

Ella, a small town nestled amidst dramatic peaks, was a highlight of the trip. Hiking up to Ella Rock rewarded me with panoramic views that stretched to the horizon, a patchwork of emerald green fields and cascading waterfalls. The Nine Arches Bridge, an engineering marvel from the colonial era, provided a perfect photo opportunity as I watched the iconic blue train rumble through.

No journey to Sri Lanka is complete without experiencing its wildlife. Yala National Park offered thrilling safaris where I glimpsed leopards prowling through the underbrush and elephants bathing in watering holes. Udawalawe National Park, renowned for its elephant population, allowed for intimate encounters with these gentle giants against a backdrop of golden sunsets.

The cultural immersion continued with visits to Kandy, the cultural capital. The Temple of the Tooth Relic, nestled beside a tranquil lake, held centuries of Buddhist heritage within its sacred walls. Attending a traditional Kandyan dance performance, with its vibrant costumes and rhythmic drumming, left me spellbound.

Heading south, the coastal town of Galle captivated me with its Dutch-colonial charm. Strolling along the fort ramparts, I marveled at the blend of European and Sri Lankan architectural styles. The cobblestone streets lined with boutiques and cafes offered a perfect respite before heading to Mirissa for a memorable whale watching excursion.

Sri Lanka's culinary delights were a constant delight throughout my journey. From spicy seafood curries to delectable hoppers and the ubiquitous roti stalls, each meal was a feast for the senses. Sampling Ceylon tea-infused cuisine in a traditional home-cooked meal provided insights into the island's gastronomic heritage.

As my journey through Sri Lanka drew to a close, I reflected on the warmth and hospitality of its people. Whether sipping coconut water on a sun-drenched beach or sharing stories with locals over a cup of aromatic Ceylon tea, I felt a deep connection to this enchanting island.

Sri Lanka, with its blend of history, natural beauty, and cultural diversity, has woven itself into my heart. Each moment, from ancient ruins to misty mountains and bustling markets, had left an indelible mark. As I bid farewell to this island paradise, I carried with me not just memories, but a profound appreciation for the rich tapestry of experiences that Sri Lanka had offered me.

Sri Lanka Population

Population: Sri Lanka has a population of approximately 24 million people (2023 estimate).

Population Growth: The population growth rate is moderate, with an annual increase estimated at around 0.71%.

Population Density: Sri Lanka's population density is relatively high at about 341 people per square kilometer, reflecting its small geographic size and concentrated settlement patterns.

Urbanization: Around 18% of the population lives in urban areas, with major cities like Colombo (the capital), Kandy, Galle, and Jaffna being significant urban centers.

These demographic insights provide a snapshot of Sri Lanka's population, reflecting its diversity and the demographic dynamics shaping the country's social and economic landscape.

Chapter 1: Sri Lanka, The True Gem of the world

Sri Lanka, known as "The True Gem of the World," boasts stunning landscapes, rich cultural heritage, and diverse wildlife, making it a must-visit destination for travelers.

What Makes Sri Lanka a Famous Tourist Paradise

Sri Lanka is a popular tourist destination, and here are some of the top reasons why:

Stunning Beaches

Sri Lanka boasts beautiful beaches with clear blue waters. From the lively shores of Bentota to the tranquil sands of Mirissa, there's something for every beach lover.

Rich History

The country is home to ancient cities and UNESCO World Heritage sites like Sigiriya, Anuradhapura, and Polonnaruwa. These places offer a glimpse into Sri Lanka's fascinating past.

Diverse Wildlife
Sri Lanka is a haven for wildlife enthusiasts. You can visit national parks like Yala and Udawalawe to see elephants, leopards, and a variety of bird species.

Delicious Cuisine
Sri Lankan food is a delightful mix of flavors. Don't miss trying local dishes like rice and curry, hoppers, and seafood specialties.

Scenic Landscapes
From the rolling tea plantations in Nuwara Eliya to the lush rainforests of Sinharaja, Sri Lanka's natural beauty is breathtaking. The scenic train rides, especially the one from Kandy to Ella, offer spectacular views.

Adventure Activities
For adventure seekers, Sri Lanka offers surfing, diving, hiking, and even hot air ballooning. Spots like Arugam Bay are famous for surfing, while the central highlands provide excellent hiking trails.

These are just a few reasons why Sri Lanka is a beloved tourist paradise. Its diverse attractions cater to all kinds of travelers, ensuring a memorable experience for everyone.

Who would benefit from visiting Sri Lanka?

Visiting Sri Lanka can be a great experience for a variety of travelers. Here's who would benefit the most:

Beach Lovers

If you love the beach, Sri Lanka's stunning coastlines, with both bustling beaches and secluded spots, are perfect for you.

History Buffs

History enthusiasts will enjoy exploring ancient cities, historic temples, and UNESCO World Heritage sites that tell the story of Sri Lanka's rich past.

Wildlife Enthusiasts
Nature and wildlife lovers can experience safaris in national parks, where they can see elephants, leopards, and diverse bird species.

Foodies
Sri Lanka is a paradise for food lovers, offering a variety of flavorful dishes, fresh seafood, and unique local delicacies.

Sri Lanka offers something for everyone, making it an ideal destination for a wide range of travelers looking for unique and memorable experiences.

Desirable Locations for first time visitors in Sri Lanka

If you're visiting Sri Lanka for the first time, here are some must-see locations:

Colombo
As the capital city, Colombo offers a mix of modern life, colonial buildings, and vibrant

markets. Don't miss the Galle Face Green, Colombo Fort, and the National Museum.

Kandy
Located in the central highlands, Kandy is home to the Temple of the Tooth Relic and the beautiful Kandy Lake. The annual Esala Perahera festival is a major highlight.

Sigiriya
This ancient rock fortress is a UNESCO World Heritage site and offers stunning views from the top. The surrounding gardens and frescoes are also worth exploring.

Ella
A charming hill town, Ella is known for its scenic train rides, tea plantations, and hiking trails, including the popular trek to Ella Rock and the Nine Arches Bridge.

Galle
Galle's historic fort area is another UNESCO World Heritage site. Wander through its

cobblestone streets, visit the lighthouse, and explore the many boutiques and cafes.

Mirissa

Perfect for beach lovers, Mirissa offers beautiful beaches, whale watching tours, and a relaxed atmosphere. It's a great spot to unwind by the sea.

Anuradhapura

One of Sri Lanka's ancient capitals, Anuradhapura is famous for its well-preserved ruins of an ancient Sri Lankan civilization. The sacred Bodhi tree and numerous stupas are key attractions.

These locations provide a fantastic introduction to Sri Lanka's diverse attractions, from cultural heritage and historical sites to natural beauty and wildlife.

Chapter 2: Planning a Journey to Sri Lanka

Planning a trip to Sri Lanka includes stunning beaches, rich history, diverse wildlife, delicious cuisine, vibrant festivals, and warm hospitality, offering memorable experiences for all types of travelers.

What is the optimal period for traveling to Sri Lanka

The optimal period for traveling to Sri Lanka depends on the region you plan to visit and your preferences:

December to March (High Season)
- *Weather:* Dry and sunny weather across the island.
- *Activities:* Ideal for beach holidays, wildlife safaris, and cultural exploration.
- *Events:* Festivals like Sinhala and Tamil New Year in April.

April and September (Shoulder Seasons)
- *Weather:* Transitional months with mixed weather, but still pleasant.
- *Crowds:* Fewer tourists compared to peak season.
- *Activities:* Good for sightseeing and exploring central highlands.

May to August (Southwest Monsoon)
- *Weather:* Southwest monsoon brings rain to the southwest coast and hill country.
- *Activities:* Northern and eastern beaches are ideal during this period.
- *Events:* Esala Perahera festival in Kandy in July/August.

October and November (Inter-monsoon Period)
- *Weather:* Inter-monsoon rains occur sporadically; generally, weather is fair.
- *Activities:* Suitable for visiting cultural sites and enjoying quieter beaches.
- *Events:* Deepavali (Diwali) celebrations in October.

Choose your travel time based on the activities you prefer and the regions you plan to explore in Sri Lanka.

Month by Month Weather in Sri Lanka

Here's a detailed breakdown of the month-by-month weather in Sri Lanka including temperature ranges:

- ❖ **January**
- Weather: Dry and sunny.
- Temperatures: Coastal areas average highs of 30-32°C (86-90°F), cooler in hill country.
- Activities: Ideal for beach visits, wildlife safaris, and exploring cultural sites.

- ❖ **February**
- Weather: Continued dry and sunny weather.
- Temperatures: Coastal areas average highs of 30-32°C (86-90°F), cooler in hill country.
- Activities: Great for outdoor activities, sightseeing, and enjoying festivals.

❖ March
- Weather: Dry with clear skies.
- Temperatures: Coastal areas average highs of 31-33°C (88-91°F), cooler in hill country.
- Activities: Perfect for beach holidays, hiking, and cultural tours.

❖ April
- Weather: Transition to inter-monsoon period with occasional showers.
- Temperatures: Coastal areas average highs of 31-33°C (88-91°F), cooler in hill country.
- Activities: Good for exploring central highlands and quieter beach spots.

❖ May
- Weather: Increasing humidity with occasional showers.
- Temperatures: Coastal areas average highs of 31-33°C (88-91°F), cooler in hill country.
- Activities: Ideal for cultural exploration and visiting less crowded sites.

❖ **June**
- Weather: Southwest monsoon begins, affecting the southwest coast and hill country.
- Temperatures: Coastal areas average highs of 30-32°C (86-90°F), cooler in hill country.
- Activities: Best for exploring northern and eastern beaches, cultural festivals.

❖ **July**
- Weather: Southwest monsoon continues.
- Temperatures: Coastal areas average highs of 29-31°C (84-88°F), cooler in hill country.
- Activities: Focus on indoor cultural activities, northern and eastern coastal visits.

❖ **August**
- Weather: Southwest monsoon persists.
- Temperatures: Coastal areas average highs of 29-31°C (84-88°F), cooler in hill country.
- Activities: Best for wildlife safaris, rainforest exploration, and eastern coast visits.

❖ September
- Weather: Southwest monsoon gradually subsides.
- Temperatures: Coastal areas average highs of 29-31°C (84-88°F), cooler in hill country.
- Activities: Ideal for quieter beach vacations and cultural tours.

❖ October
- Weather: Inter-monsoon period with sporadic rains.
- Temperatures: Coastal areas average highs of 30-32°C (86-90°F), cooler in hill country.
- Activities: Suitable for visiting cultural sites and enjoying quieter beach locations.

❖ November
- Weather: Inter-monsoon continues with occasional showers.
- Temperatures: Coastal areas average highs of 30-32°C (86-90°F), cooler in hill country.
- Activities: Good for exploring nature reserves, historic sites, and coastal areas.

❖ **December**
- Weather: Transition to dry season begins.
- Temperatures: Coastal areas average highs of 30-32°C (86-90°F), cooler in hill country.
- Activities: Perfect for beach holidays, wildlife safaris, and outdoor adventures.

These temperature ranges can help you plan your trip to Sri Lanka according to your comfort level with heat and humidity.

How to Journey to Sri Lanka

Explore Sri Lanka via flights from major international airports, connecting through Colombo's Bandaranaike Airport, or cruise ships docking at Colombo Port.

Air Travel to Sri Lanka: Expenses and Costs

Air travel expenses to Sri Lanka vary based on factors like departure city, travel class, and booking time:

Economy Class
- *Average Cost:* Prices range from $500 to $1,200 round-trip.
- *Booking Tips:* Booking 2-3 months in advance often yields the best deals.
- *Additional Costs:* Optional upgrades for extra legroom or meals.

Business Class
- *Average Cost:* Prices typically range from $1,500 to $3,000 round-trip.
- *Booking Tips:* Book early for discounts; last-minute upgrades can be costly.

Factors Influencing Costs
- *Seasonal Variations:* High season (December-March) can increase prices.
- *Flight Duration:* Direct flights are more expensive than connecting ones.
- *Departure City:* Flights from major hubs (e.g., London, New York) tend to be pricier.

Additional Expenses
- ***Visa Fees:*** Range from $20 to $100 depending on nationality.
- ***Airport Transfers:*** Taxis cost about $20 to Colombo from Bandaranaike Airport.
- ***Travel Insurance:*** Recommended; prices vary based on coverage and duration.

Understanding these costs helps plan a budget-friendly trip to Sri Lanka via air travel, ensuring a comfortable and enjoyable journey.

Road Travel to Sri Lanka and its Expenses
Road travel in Sri Lanka primarily involves renting a car or hiring a driver, with considerations for expenses and costs:

Renting a Car
- ***Costs:*** Daily rates start at approximately $30-$50 USD for a basic car.
- ***Insurance:*** Additional cost for comprehensive coverage; check rental terms.
- ***Fuel:*** Gasoline prices vary; budget around $10-$15 USD per day for fuel.

- Road Conditions: Generally good on major routes; rural areas may have narrower roads.

Hiring a Driver
- ***Costs:*** Prices range from $40-$80 USD per day, depending on vehicle type and itinerary.
- ***Inclusions:*** Driver's fee typically covers fuel and insurance.
- ***Benefits:*** Local expertise, navigation assistance, and convenience.

Understanding these expenses helps plan for road travel in Sri Lanka, offering flexibility and convenience to explore the island's diverse landscapes and attractions.

Traveling to Sri Lanka by Sea: Process and Costs

Traveling to Sri Lanka by sea primarily involves cruise ships or private yachts, with considerations for process and costs:

Cruise Ships
- ***Process:*** Arrive at Colombo Port; disembarkation involves customs and immigration procedures.
- ***Costs:*** Prices vary widely based on cruise duration, cabin class, and amenities.
- ***Visa:*** Cruise lines may assist with visa arrangements; check requirements beforehand.

Private Yachts
- ***Process:*** Dock at designated ports; clearance involves customs, immigration, and port authorities.
- ***Costs:*** Entry fees and port charges vary; inquire about fees before arrival.
- ***Visa:*** Crew and passengers must have appropriate visas; arrange in advance.

Tips for Sea Travel
- ***Documentation:*** Ensure passports, visas, and yacht papers are in order before arrival.
- ***Local Regulations:*** Follow customs and port regulations for smooth entry and departure.

- *Local Currency:* Have local currency for expenses ashore; major credit cards may be accepted.

Understanding these processes and costs helps prepare for a sea journey to Sri Lanka, ensuring a seamless and enjoyable maritime experience.

Prominent Tourist Destinations for Accommodation in Sri Lanka

Sri Lanka offers a range of prominent tourist destinations with diverse accommodation options:

Colombo
- *Hotels:* Luxury options like Shangri-La Colombo and Hilton Colombo.
- *Boutique Stays:* Unique stays in historic buildings and modern boutiques.

Kandy
- *Resorts:* Mahaweli Reach Hotel and Earl's Regency Hotel.

- *Guesthouses:* Affordable options with local charm near cultural sites.

Galle
- *Fort Area:* Boutique hotels like Amangalla and Fort Bazaar.
- Beachside: Resorts with ocean views along Unawatuna and Thalpe beaches.

Nuwara Eliya
- *Colonial Charm:* Grand Hotel and Heritance Tea Factory.
- *Tea Estates:* Stay amidst lush plantations offering scenic views.

Mirissa
- *Beach Resorts:* Sri Sharavi Beach Villas and Spa, Lantern Boutique Hotel.
- *Guesthouses:* Budget-friendly options near Mirissa Beach.

Ella
- *Mountain Views:* 98 Acres Resort and Spa, Ella Jungle Resort.

- ***Homestays:*** Authentic local experiences in tranquil surroundings.

These destinations cater to various preferences, from luxury seekers to budget travelers, ensuring a comfortable and memorable stay in Sri Lanka.

Essential Packing Guide for Your Journey to Sri Lanka

Packing for your trip to Sri Lanka involves considering the climate, activities, and cultural norms. Here's an essential packing guide:

Clothing

- ***Lightweight Clothes:*** Cotton or linen for hot and humid weather.
- ***Swimwear:*** For beaches and pools.
- ***Modest Attire:*** Long pants, skirts, and shirts for temples and cultural sites.
- ***Jacket/Sweater:*** Light jacket for cooler hill country areas like Nuwara Eliya.

Footwear

- ***Comfortable Walking Shoes:*** For sightseeing and hiking.
- ***Sandals/Flip-Flops:*** For beaches and casual wear.
- ***Dress Shoes:*** If planning to dine in upscale restaurants.

Accessories

- ***Hat/Cap:*** To protect from the sun.
- ***Sunglasses:*** UV protection for sunny days.
- ***Scarf/Shawl:*** Useful for temple visits and cool evenings.

Toiletries and Health

- ***Sunscreen:*** High SPF to protect against strong sun.
- ***Insect Repellent:*** Especially for evenings and rural areas.
- ***Basic First Aid Kit:*** Band-aids, antiseptic cream, and any personal medications.
- ***Hand Sanitizer:*** For hygiene on the go.

Electronics

- *Camera/Smartphone:* To capture your experiences.
- *Chargers/Adapters:* Sri Lanka uses Type D and G plug types; voltage is 230V.
- *Power Bank:* For charging devices on the move.

Travel Documents

- *Passport/Visa:* Ensure they are valid and up-to-date.
- *Travel Insurance:* Coverage for health, travel delays, and theft.
- *Copies of Documents:* Keep digital and physical copies of important documents.

Money and Security

- *Cash:* Local currency (Sri Lankan Rupee) for small purchases.
- *Credit/Debit Cards:* Widely accepted in urban areas.
- *Money Belt/Pouch:* To keep valuables secure.

This comprehensive packing list ensures you're well-prepared for a comfortable and enjoyable journey to Sri Lanka.

Crafting Your Ideal Itinerary: How Long to Stay in Sri Lanka

Crafting your ideal itinerary for Sri Lanka depends on your interests and the experiences you want to enjoy. Here are some suggestions based on popular attractions and activities:

Short Trip (5-7 Days)
- *Highlights:* Visit Colombo, explore Kandy's cultural sites, and see the Sigiriya Rock Fortress.
- *Activities:* Take a scenic train ride to Ella, relax on the beaches of Mirissa or Unawatuna.
- *Recommended:* Ideal for a quick cultural immersion and beach relaxation.

Medium Trip (10-14 Days)
- *Highlights:* Include Anuradhapura and Polonnaruwa for ancient ruins, Yala National Park for wildlife.

- *Activities:* Explore the tea plantations in Nuwara Eliya, visit Galle's historic fort, and relax in Bentota.
- *Recommended:* Allows for a deeper exploration of Sri Lanka's cultural and natural diversity.

Extended Trip (2-3 Weeks)

- *Highlights:* Comprehensive tour covering all major regions like Jaffna in the north and Trincomalee in the east.
- *Activities:* Diving in Pigeon Island, whale watching in Mirissa, and exploring lesser-known areas like Dambulla.
- *Recommended:* Provides ample time for in-depth exploration and relaxation at various destinations.

Planning the duration of your stay in Sri Lanka ensures a balanced and enriching travel experience, tailored to your preferences and interests.

Chapter 3: Understanding Sri Lanka Entry Requirements: A Comprehensive Guide

Understanding Sri Lanka's entry requirements ensures smooth travel: visas, vaccinations, and documentation tailored to your trip are essential for hassle-free entry.

Visa Types for Sri Lanka visitors

Here are the details of visa types available for visitors to Sri Lanka:

Tourist Visa

- **Duration:** Allows for stays up to 30 days, extendable up to 180 days.
- **Application:** Apply online through the Electronic Travel Authorization (ETA) system or at Sri Lankan embassies/consulates.
- **Cost:** Fees vary; typically around $20-$100 USD depending on nationality and processing method.

- *Requirements:* Passport validity of at least six months, return ticket, and proof of sufficient funds.

Business Visa

- *Duration:* Generally valid for stays up to 30 days, extendable for longer periods.
- *Application:* Apply through Sri Lankan embassies/consulates or online via ETA system.
- *Requirements:* Invitation from a business entity in Sri Lanka, proof of business activities, and other standard visa application documents.

Transit Visa

- *Duration:* Valid for a short period (usually 2-3 days).
- *Application:* Apply through Sri Lankan embassies/consulates or online via the ETA system.
- *Cost:* Fees vary; generally lower than tourist visas.
- *Requirements:* Proof of onward travel, valid visa for the destination country, and other transit-specific documents.

Electronic Travel Authorization (ETA)

- **Duration:** Allows short visits up to 30 days.
- **Application:** Apply online through the official ETA website or through authorized travel agents.
- **Cost:** Fees vary; typically around $20-$35 USD depending on nationality.
- **Requirements:** Passport validity of at least six months, return ticket, and proof of sufficient funds.

Understanding these visa types helps travelers plan their entry into Sri Lanka effectively, ensuring compliance with immigration regulations and a smooth travel experience.

Proof of Accommodation in Sri Lanka

Proof of accommodation in Sri Lanka is typically required as part of visa applications or immigration procedures. Here's what you need to know:

Types of Proof Accepted:

Hotel Reservations: Booking confirmations from hotels, resorts, guesthouses, or hostels.

Rental Agreements: For those staying in vacation rentals, apartments, or villas, a rental agreement or booking confirmation is necessary.

Invitation Letters: If staying with friends or family, a signed invitation letter with details of accommodation provided by the host.

Submission:

- ***Visa Applications:*** Attach proof of accommodation when applying for a visa through embassies, consulates, or online systems like the Electronic Travel Authorization (ETA) system.

- ***Immigration Check:*** Immigration officials may request proof of accommodation upon arrival in Sri Lanka.

Having valid proof of accommodation ensures compliance with entry requirements and a smoother travel experience in Sri Lanka.

Proof of Financial Capability for Traveling to Sri Lanka

Proof of financial capability for traveling to Sri Lanka typically includes demonstrating sufficient funds to cover your expenses during your stay. Here's how you can provide proof:

Accepted Forms of Proof:

Bank Statements: Showing sufficient funds in your account for the duration of your stay.

Credit Card Statements: Showing available credit or recent transactions.

Traveler's Checks: Evidence of purchased traveler's checks.

Salary Slips or Income Proof: If employed, provide recent salary slips or income statements.

Submission:

- ***Visa Applications:*** Attach financial documents as required by the Sri Lankan embassy or consulate.

- ***Immigration Check:*** Have these documents available for inspection upon arrival in Sri Lanka.

Showing proof of financial capability helps ensure compliance with entry requirements and a smooth travel experience in Sri Lanka.

Chapter 4: Lodging Choices and Expenses in Sri Lanka

Choosing lodging in Sri Lanka offers a range of options to suit different preferences and budgets:

Hotels and Resorts

- *Luxury:* Prices range from $150 to $500+ USD per night.
   - *Features:* High-end amenities, spa services, beachfront locations.
   - *Examples:* Shangri-La Colombo, Anantara Peace Haven Tangalle Resort.

- Mid-Range: Prices range from $50 to $150 USD per night.
   - *Features:* Comfortable rooms, swimming pools, restaurants.
   - *Examples:* Cinnamon Bey Beruwala, Jetwing Beach Negombo.

- Budget: Prices range from $20 to $50 USD per night.
   - *Features:* Basic accommodations, clean rooms, sometimes include breakfast.

- *Examples:* Hotel J, Clock Inn Colombo.

Guesthouses and Homestays

- *Local Guesthouses:* Prices range from $15 to $40 USD per night.
  - *Features:* Cozy atmosphere, personalized service, local breakfast.
  - *Examples:* Villa Araliya, Hilltop Guesthouse Ella.

- *Homestays:* Prices vary; typically $10 to $30 USD per night.
  - *Features:* Stay with a local family, experience local culture and cuisine.
  - *Examples:* Ella Okreech Cottages, Amma's Home Stay Galle.

Boutique and Eco-Lodges

- *Boutique Hotels:* Prices range from $80 to $200 USD per night.
  - *Features:* Unique designs, personalized service, often in scenic locations.
  - *Examples:* Fort Bazaar, The Last House Tangalle.

- ***Eco-Lodges:*** Prices vary; typically $50 to $150 USD per night.
    - **Features:** Sustainable practices, nature-focused activities.
    - ***Examples:*** Jetwing Kaduruketha, Rainforest Eco Lodge Sinharaja.

Additional Expenses:
- ***Meals:*** Budget around $5 to $15 USD per meal at local restaurants.
- ***Transport:*** Tuk-tuks or taxis for short trips; longer trips may require private drivers or buses.

Choosing lodging in Sri Lanka offers diverse experiences from beachfront luxury to immersive homestays, catering to every traveler's preferences and budget.

Hotel Bookings and Tips in Sri Lanka

Booking hotels in Sri Lanka can be straightforward with these tips to ensure a smooth experience:

Booking Platforms

- **Online Platforms:** Use trusted websites like Booking.com, Agoda, or Expedia for a wide range of options and reviews.
- **Hotel Websites:** Direct bookings often offer promotions and loyalty rewards.

Choosing Hotels

- **Location:** Consider proximity to attractions, transportation hubs, or beaches depending on your itinerary.
- **Reviews:** Read recent guest reviews to gauge cleanliness, service, and facilities.
- **Facilities:** Check for amenities like Wi-Fi, breakfast, swimming pools, and air conditioning.

Budget Considerations

- **Seasonal Rates:** Prices may fluctuate; book in advance for better deals, especially during peak seasons.
- **Room Types:** Compare prices for standard rooms, suites, or family rooms based on your needs.

- ***Cancellation Policies:*** Understand cancellation fees and deadlines; opt for flexible bookings if your plans may change.

Additional Tips

- ***Contact Hotels:*** For specific requests or to confirm details before booking.
- ***Local Insights:*** Ask locals or online forums for recommendations based on your preferences.
- ***Payment:*** Use secure methods like credit cards or PayPal for online bookings.

Example Hotels in Sri Lanka

- ***Luxury:*** Shangri-La Colombo, Anantara Peace Haven Tangalle Resort.
- ***Mid-Range:*** Cinnamon Bey Beruwala, Jetwing Beach Negombo.
- ***Budget:*** Hotel J Colombo, Clock Inn Colombo.

Booking hotels in Sri Lanka ensures you find accommodations that meet your needs, whether you're seeking luxury, comfort, or budget-friendly options during your stay.

Luxury Hotels in Sri Lanka

Luxury hotels in Sri Lanka offer exquisite accommodations and top-notch amenities. Here are details on some of the finest luxury hotels:

❖ **Shangri-La Hotel, Colombo**
- *Location:* Prime location in Colombo overlooking the Indian Ocean.
- *Rooms:* Elegant rooms and suites with city or ocean views.
- *Amenities:* Spa, outdoor pool, multiple dining options including rooftop bar.
- *Highlights:* Close to Galle Face Green and upscale shopping areas.
- *Website:* [Shangri-La Hotel, Colombo](https://www.shangri-la.com/colombo/shangrila/)

❖ **Anantara Peace Haven Tangalle Resort**
- *Location:* Tranquil beachfront setting near Tangalle.
- *Accommodation:* Luxurious villas and rooms with private pools and ocean views.

- *Facilities:* Spa, infinity pool, fitness center, and multiple dining options.
- *Activities:* Yoga, cooking classes, and water sports available.
- *Website:* [Anantara Peace Haven Tangalle Resort](https://www.anantara.com/en/peace-haven-tangalle)

❖ Cape Weligama

- *Location:* Cliff-top resort overlooking Weligama Bay.
- *Accommodation:* Spacious villas and suites with private plunge pools.
- *Facilities:* Infinity pools, spa, fitness center, and gourmet dining.
- *Activities:* Surfing, whale watching, and cultural excursions.
- *Website:* [Cape Weligama](https://www.resplendentceylon.com/capeweligama)

❖ Amanwella

- *Location:* Secluded beachfront resort near Tangalle.

- *Accommodation:* Contemporary suites with private plunge pools and ocean views.
- *Facilities:* Spa, infinity pool, beach club, and fine dining restaurant.
- *Activities:* Yoga, wildlife safaris, and visits to local temples.
-*Website:*[Amanwella](https://www.aman.com/resorts/amanwella)

❖ **Jetwing Vil Uyana**

- *Location:* Eco-luxury resort near Sigiriya with views of the ancient rock fortress.
- *Accommodation:* Luxury villas and dwellings amidst a wetland sanctuary.
- *Facilities:* Spa, infinity pool, bird-watching, and organic dining experiences.
- *Activities:* Cultural tours, nature walks, and wildlife safaris.
-*Website:*[Jetwing Vil Uyana](https://www.jetwinghotels.com/jetwingviluyana/)

Booking Tips:
- **Book Direct:** Check hotel websites for promotions, packages, and loyalty rewards.
- **Seasonal Rates:** Prices may vary; consider off-peak seasons for better deals.
- **Special Requests:** Contact hotels directly for special occasions or specific needs.

These luxury hotels in Sri Lanka offer exceptional experiences amidst stunning natural landscapes, ensuring a memorable stay with world-class hospitality and amenities.

Cheap and affordable Hotels in Sri Lanka

Finding affordable hotels in Sri Lanka can provide budget-conscious travelers with comfortable accommodations. Here are some options:

Clock Inn Colombo
- **Location:** Central Colombo, close to attractions and transportation hubs.
- **Features:** Dormitory-style and private rooms, free Wi-Fi, common lounge area.

- ***Price:*** Budget-friendly, typically around $15-$30 USD per night.
- ***Website:*** [Clock Inn Colombo](http://www.clockinn.lk/colombo/)

Hotel J Colombo

- **Location:** Conveniently located in Colombo with easy access to shopping and dining.
- **Features:** Comfortable rooms, breakfast included, rooftop terrace.
- **Price:** Moderate prices, generally between $30-$50 USD per night.
- Website: [Hotel J Colombo](https://www.hotelj.lk/)

Hangover Hostels Colombo

- **Location:** Vibrant area in Colombo, ideal for budget travelers and backpackers.
- **Features**: Dormitory-style rooms, communal kitchen, social lounge area.
- **Price:** Budget-friendly, typically around $10-$20 USD per night.
- Website: [Hangover Hostels Colombo](https://hangoverhostels.com/)

My Little Island Hostel, Galle

- Location: Close to Galle Fort and beaches in Galle.
- Features: Dormitory-style rooms, shared bathrooms, breakfast available.
- Price: Affordable rates, generally around $10-$25 USD per night.
- Website: [My Little Island Hostel](https://www.mylittleislandhostel.com/)

Blue Lanka Hostel, Ella

- Location: Scenic Ella, popular for hiking and nature enthusiasts.
- Features: Dormitory and private rooms, shared kitchen, friendly atmosphere.
- Price: Budget-friendly, typically around $10-$30 USD per night.
- Website: [Blue Lanka Hostel](https://www.bluelanka.com/)

Booking Tips:

- Online Platforms: Use Booking.com, Hostelworld, or Agoda for reviews and easy booking.
- Reviews: Check recent guest reviews for cleanliness, location, and value for money.
- Location: Consider proximity to attractions and public transportation for convenience.

These affordable hotels and hostels in Sri Lanka cater to travelers looking to explore the country on a budget, offering basic amenities and a comfortable stay without breaking the bank.

Romantic hotels in Sri Lanka

For couples seeking romantic hotels in Sri Lanka, here are some enchanting options known for their ambiance and luxurious amenities:

Cape Weligama
- Location: Overlooking Weligama Bay on the southern coast.
- Accommodation: Spacious villas and suites with private plunge pools.

- Romantic Features: Stunning ocean views, candlelit dinners, and private dining experiences.
- Activities: Couples' spa treatments, private beach access, and sunset cruises.
- Website: [Cape Weligama](https://www.resplendentceylon.com/capeweligama)

Anantara Peace Haven Tangalle Resort
- Location: Secluded beachfront setting near Tangalle.
- Accommodation: Elegant rooms and villas with ocean views and private pools.
- Romantic Features: Spa treatments for couples, private dining on the beach, and romantic excursions.
- Activities: Yoga sessions, cooking classes, and nature walks.
- Website: [Anantara Peace Haven Tangalle Resort](https://www.anantara.com/en/peace-haven-tangalle)

Uga Chena Huts, Yala

- Location: Amidst the wilderness near Yala National Park.
- Accommodation: Luxurious huts with private plunge pools and jungle views.
- Romantic Features: Secluded setting, outdoor rain showers, and intimate dining experiences.
- Activities: Safari adventures, spa treatments, and stargazing.
- Website: [Uga Chena Huts](https://www.ugaescapes.com/chena-huts/)

Jetwing Lighthouse, Galle
- Location: Overlooking the Indian Ocean in historic Galle.
- Accommodation: Stylish rooms and suites with ocean or garden views.
- Romantic Features: Sunset cocktails by the pool, fine dining with ocean views, and couples' spa treatments.
- Activities: Galle Fort exploration, whale watching, and beach walks.
- Website: [Jetwing Lighthouse](https://www.jetwinghotels.com/jetwinglighthouse/)

Tri Lanka, Koggala Lake
- Location: Eco-friendly resort on Koggala Lake.
- Accommodation: Sustainable design villas with lake views.
- Romantic Features: Infinity pool, yoga pavilion, and organic farm-to-table dining.
- Activities: Boat rides on the lake, spa treatments, and cooking classes.
- Website: [Tri Lanka](https://www.trilanka.com/)

Tips for Romantic Stays:
- Special Touches: Look for hotels offering honeymoon packages or special romantic amenities.
- Advance Booking: Reserve early for the best rooms and rates, especially during peak seasons.
- Local Experiences: Explore nearby attractions and cultural sites for memorable outings together.

These romantic hotels in Sri Lanka promise a magical getaway with luxurious accommodations, scenic views, and intimate experiences tailored for couples.

Camping and Glamping in Sri Lanka by Tourists

Camping and glamping in Sri Lanka offer unique ways for tourists to connect with nature. Here's what you need to know:

Camping Options

Camping in National Parks
   - Locations: Yala National Park, Udawalawe National Park, Horton Plains National Park.
   - Facilities: Basic campsites with tents or safari lodges.
   - Activities: Wildlife safaris, birdwatching, and nature walks.
   - Permits: Required; arrange through park authorities or tour operators.

Beach Camping
   - Locations: Trincomalee, Arugam Bay, Kalpitiya.
   - Facilities: Tents or beachside cabins.

- Activities: Snorkeling, diving, beach walks, and cultural experiences.
- Local Operators: Offer packages with equipment and guides.

Glamping Experiences

Luxury Tented Camps
- Locations: Knuckles Mountain Range, Ella, Sigiriya.
- Accommodations: Lavish tents with comfortable beds, en-suite bathrooms, and private decks.
- Facilities: Gourmet dining, spa treatments, and personalized services.
- Activities: Hiking, cultural tours, and wellness activities.

Eco-Friendly Glamping
- Locations: Kandalama, Dambulla, Koggala.
- Accommodations: Sustainable lodges or eco-retreats with unique designs.
- Facilities: Organic dining, yoga sessions, and nature-inspired experiences.

- Activities: Birdwatching, lake kayaking, and farm visits.

Tips for Camping and Glamping
- Season: Plan during the dry season (December to April) for better weather.
- Permits: Check and obtain necessary permits in advance, especially for national parks.
- Pack Essentials: Bring insect repellent, comfortable clothing, and sturdy footwear.
- Local Guidance: Use local tour operators for safety and authentic experiences.

Camping and glamping in Sri Lanka offer adventurous and luxurious ways to experience its diverse landscapes and rich biodiversity, catering to both nature enthusiasts and those seeking unique accommodations.

Chapter 5: Nightlife and Dining Etiquette in Sri Lanka

Nightlife in Sri Lanka offers vibrant experiences with diverse dining options. Respect local customs like removing shoes before entering homes and using your right hand for eating.

Sri Lanka Nightlife

Sri Lanka's nightlife offers a blend of cultural experiences and modern entertainment, catering to diverse tastes across its cities and coastal towns:

Colombo Nightlife

- **Highlights:** Vibrant bars, clubs, and casinos.
- **Locations:** Colombo 7, Colombo 3 (Kollupitiya), and Galle Face Green.
- **Venues:** Sky Lounge, Colombo Courtyard, and Bally's Casino.
- Activities: Live music, DJ performances, and themed parties.

Beachside Destinations
- **Locations:** Unawatuna, Hikkaduwa, and Mirissa.
- **Venues:** Beach bars, seafood restaurants, and beach parties.
- **Activities:** Bonfires, beachside cocktails, and sunset views.

Cultural Shows
- **Locations:** Kandy and Colombo.
- **Venues:** Nelum Pokuna Mahinda Rajapaksa Theatre and Kandyan Dance performances.
- **Activities:** Traditional dance, music, and storytelling.

Casual Hangouts
- **Locations:** Ella, Nuwara Eliya, and Galle.
- **Venues:** Rooftop bars, tea lounges, and local pubs.
- **Activities:** Relaxed ambiance, craft beers, and scenic views.

Tips for Enjoying Sri Lanka Nightlife:
- **Dress Code:** Check venue requirements; smart-casual attire is often preferred.
- **Local Customs:** Respect cultural norms; avoid public displays of affection.
- **Safety:** Use reputable transportation services and keep belongings secure.
- **Timing:** Nightlife typically starts late; plan for late evenings and early mornings.

Sri Lanka's nightlife scene caters to both locals and tourists, offering a mix of modern entertainment and traditional cultural experiences, ensuring there's something for everyone to enjoy after sunset.

Must Try Sri Lanka Food And Cuisines

Sri Lankan cuisine offers a delightful array of flavors and dishes influenced by its rich cultural heritage. Here are some must-try foods:

Rice and Curry
- **Description:** A staple dish featuring rice served with various curries, including chicken,

fish, or vegetable, often accompanied by dhal (lentil curry), sambal (spicy condiment), and papadam (crispy flatbread).

Kottu Roti
- **Description:** Chopped roti stir-fried with vegetables, egg, and a choice of meat (chicken, beef, or mutton), seasoned with spices and sometimes served with a side of curry sauce.

Hoppers (Appa)
- **Description:** Bowl-shaped pancakes made from fermented rice flour and coconut milk, served with a soft-cooked egg in the center (egg hopper) or with sambal and curry for savory flavors.

String Hoppers (Indiappa)
- **Description:** Thin strands of rice noodles steamed into flat, circular cakes, often served for breakfast with coconut sambal or curry.

Fish Ambul Thiyal

- **Description:** Sour fish curry made with tuna or another firm fish, cooked with goraka (Malabar tamarind), black pepper, and spices until thick and flavorful.

Lamprais

- **Description:** Dutch-inspired dish consisting of rice cooked with meat (usually chicken, beef, or pork), accompanied by fried brinjal (eggplant), blachan (shrimp paste), and a boiled egg, wrapped in banana leaf and baked.

Pol Sambol

- **Description:** Spicy coconut relish made with freshly grated coconut, red onions, chili peppers, lime juice, and salt, often served as a condiment with rice and curry.

Watalappam

- **Description:** Traditional Sri Lankan dessert similar to flan, made with coconut milk, jaggery (palm sugar), cashew nuts, eggs, and spices like cardamom and nutmeg, steamed to a smooth consistency.

Tips:
- **Local Eateries:** Visit local eateries (known as "hotels") for authentic flavors.
- **Street Food:** Try snacks like samosas, vadai (lentil cakes), and short eats from street vendors.
- **Regional Varieties:** Explore variations in dishes across different regions of Sri Lanka for diverse culinary experiences.

Enjoying Sri Lankan cuisine is not just about tasting delicious food but also experiencing the cultural richness and culinary traditions that make it unique.

Sri Lanka Famous Drinks

Sri Lanka offers a variety of refreshing and unique beverages that reflect its cultural diversity and tropical climate. Here are some famous drinks to try:

King Coconut Water
- **Description:** Refreshing and hydrating, king coconut water is harvested from young green coconuts. It's naturally sweet and packed with electrolytes, making it a popular drink to beat the heat.

Ceylon Tea
- **Description:** Renowned worldwide, Ceylon tea (or Sri Lankan tea) comes in various types including black, green, white, and oolong. Enjoy it hot or iced with milk and sugar or as a herbal infusion.

Arrack
- **Description:** A distilled alcoholic drink made from the sap of coconut flowers or sugarcane. It's often mixed with soda or enjoyed straight, offering a strong and distinct flavor.

Wood Apple Juice (Belima)
- **Description:** Made from the pulp of the wood apple fruit, this juice has a tangy-sweet flavor

with a creamy texture. It's sometimes mixed with sugar or honey for added sweetness.

Faluda
- **Description:** A popular dessert drink made with milk, rose syrup, vermicelli, basil seeds, and sometimes ice cream. It's sweet, creamy, and often garnished with nuts or fruits.

Ginger Beer
- **Description:** A non-alcoholic beverage made from fresh ginger, sugar, and carbonated water. It's spicy, slightly sweet, and a refreshing choice, especially during warm weather.

Lion Lager Beer
- **Description:** Sri Lanka's iconic beer, known for its smooth taste and moderate strength. It's widely available and enjoyed at social gatherings and bars across the country.

Falernum
- **Description:** A traditional Sri Lankan spiced syrup made from lime zest, almonds, ginger,

cloves, and sometimes rum. It's used as a mixer in cocktails or enjoyed on its own.

Tips:
- **Local Variations:** Explore regional variations and seasonal specialties.
- **Authenticity:** Try drinks from street vendors or local cafes for an authentic taste.
- **Cultural Experience:** Many drinks have cultural significance; ask locals about their favorites and traditions.

These beverages highlight Sri Lanka's rich culinary heritage and tropical ingredients, offering a diverse and enjoyable drinking experience for visitors.

Best Cafes and Restaurants in Sri Lanka

Sri Lanka boasts a vibrant culinary scene with cafes and restaurants offering diverse flavors and experiences. Here are some of the best places to dine:

Whight & Co., Colombo

- **Description:** A trendy cafe known for its specialty coffee and artisanal baked goods. Ideal for breakfast or a casual coffee break.
- **Location:** Stratford Avenue, Colombo
- Website: [Whight & Co.](https://www.whightandco.com/)

Dots Coffee, Colombo

- **Description:** Quaint cafe offering a cozy ambiance and a variety of coffee blends. Known for its relaxed atmosphere and delicious pastries.
- **Location:** Marine Drive, Colombo
-Website: [Dots Coffee](https://www.facebook.com/dotscoffee)

Barracuda Reef, Unawatuna

- **Description:** Beachfront cafe serving fresh seafood and international cuisine. Popular for its stunning ocean views and casual dining experience.
- **Location:** Unawatuna Beach, Galle.
- Website: [Barracuda Reef](https://www.barracudareef.com/)

Best Restaurants in Sri Lanka

Ministry of Crab, Colombo

- **Description:** Renowned for its crab dishes, this restaurant is a must-visit for seafood lovers. Offers a chic dining environment with a focus on quality.

- **Location:** Dutch Hospital, Colombo

- Website: [Ministry of Crab](https://www.ministryofcrab.com/)

Nuga Gama, Colombo

- **Description:** Set in a traditional village atmosphere, this restaurant serves authentic Sri Lankan cuisine buffet-style. Known for its cultural shows and hearty meals.

- **Location:** Cinnamon Grand Hotel, Colombo

- Website: [Nuga Gama](https://www.cinnamonhotels.com/cinnamongrandcolombo/dining/nuga-gama)

The Fortress Resort & Spa, Galle

- **Description:** Offers a variety of dining options including seafood grills, international

cuisine, and themed dinners. Known for its luxurious setting and ocean views.
  - **Location:** Koggala, Galle.
  - Website: [The Fortress Resort & Spa](https://www.fortressresortandspa.com/)

These cafes and restaurants in Sri Lanka promise memorable dining experiences, from casual coffee breaks to gourmet seafood dinners, catering to every palate and preference.

Sri Lanka Dining Etiquette

Dining etiquette in Sri Lanka reflects cultural norms and traditions. Here are some key points to observe:

Washing Hands: It's customary to wash hands before and after meals. Some traditional eateries may provide a pitcher of water and basin for this purpose.

Use of the Right Hand: Traditionally, meals are eaten with the right hand. The left hand is considered unclean and used for personal hygiene.

Sharing Meals: Sri Lankan meals often involve sharing dishes placed in the center of the table. It's polite to take small portions and share with others.

Respecting Elders: Elders or guests may be served first as a sign of respect. Wait for them to start eating before beginning your meal.

Removing Shoes: In some homes and traditional dining settings, removing shoes before entering is customary. Follow the lead of your host or check if shoes are kept outside.

Dress Code: Dress modestly, especially when visiting religious sites or traditional restaurants. Avoid beachwear or revealing clothing in more formal dining establishments.

Utensils: Forks and spoons are commonly used in modern restaurants. However, in more traditional settings, you may find meals eaten with hands or with cutlery provided.

Gratitude: Express gratitude for the meal by thanking the host or restaurant staff. It's appreciated to compliment the food and hospitality.

Tipping: Tipping is generally discretionary but appreciated in upscale restaurants and for good service. Check if a service charge is already included in the bill.

Alcohol Consumption: Respect local customs regarding alcohol consumption, especially in more conservative areas. In tourist areas and upscale establishments, alcohol is more widely accepted.

Observing these dining etiquettes not only shows respect for Sri Lankan culture but also enhances your dining experience, allowing you to fully enjoy the flavors and hospitality of the country.

Chapter 6: Top Attractions in Sri Lanka And Fun Activities For First Time Visitors

Explore Sri Lanka's top attractions and exciting activities for first-time visitors!

Sri Lanka landmarks

Sure, here's detailed information on each landmark:

Sigiriya: Known as the "Lion Rock," Sigiriya is an ancient rock fortress located in the central Matale District of Sri Lanka. Built by King Kashyapa in the 5th century AD, it is renowned for its impressive rock plateau that rises 200 meters above the surrounding landscape. Sigiriya is adorned with colorful frescoes, depicting celestial maidens, and a series of terraced gardens, including the famous Water Gardens. The summit offers panoramic views of the surrounding jungles and countryside.

Anuradhapura: Anuradhapura is one of Sri Lanka's ancient capitals and a UNESCO World Heritage site. Founded in the 4th century BC, it served as a center of Theravada Buddhism for many centuries. The city features numerous ancient ruins, including massive dagobas (stupas), monastic complexes, palaces, and ancient pools. The Sri Maha Bodhi, a sacred fig tree, is believed to be the oldest historically authenticated tree in the world, planted in 288 BC.

Temple of the Tooth: Located in Kandy, the Temple of the Tooth (Sri Dalada Maligawa) houses the relic of the tooth of the Buddha. It is one of the most sacred places of worship in the Buddhist world. The temple complex includes a series of smaller shrines, museums, and a golden-roofed shrine where the tooth relic is kept. The temple is an important pilgrimage site and hosts the annual Esala Perahera, a grand procession featuring dancers, drummers, and decorated elephants.

Galle Fort: Galle Fort is a well-preserved colonial-era fortification located in the southwestern coastal city of Galle. Built initially by the Portuguese in the 16th century and extensively fortified by the Dutch in the 17th century, it is a UNESCO World Heritage site. The fort's architecture reflects a blend of European styles with South Asian traditions. Within its walls are narrow streets lined with colonial buildings, boutique shops, cafes, and galleries, making it a charming area to explore.

Each of these landmarks offers a unique glimpse into Sri Lanka's history, culture, and architectural marvels, making them must-visit attractions for travelers exploring the island nation.

Sri Lanka beaches

Sri Lanka is blessed with a diverse range of beaches that cater to every type of traveler. Here are some notable ones:

Unawatuna: Known for its picturesque crescent-shaped bay, Unawatuna offers golden sands, clear waters, and excellent snorkeling opportunities. It's lively yet laid-back, with beachside cafes and bars.

Mirissa: Famous for its relaxed vibe and whale watching opportunities (best from November to April), Mirissa Beach is ideal for sunbathing, surfing, and enjoying fresh seafood at beachfront restaurants.

Bentota: Located in the southwest, Bentota Beach is known for its calm waters, making it perfect for swimming and water sports like jet skiing and windsurfing. It's also home to luxury resorts offering spa treatments and scenic boat rides on the Bentota River.

Arugam Bay: A paradise for surfers, Arugam Bay on the east coast is renowned for its consistent waves from April to October. It also boasts a laid-back atmosphere, perfect for chilling in beachfront cafes and exploring nearby lagoons and wildlife parks.

Trincomalee: Located on the northeast coast, Trincomalee features pristine beaches such as Nilaveli and Uppuveli. These beaches offer soft white sands, crystal-clear waters, and opportunities for diving to explore coral reefs and marine life.

Hikkaduwa: Known for its vibrant coral reefs and marine biodiversity, Hikkaduwa Beach is popular among snorkelers and divers. It also has a lively beach scene with beach parties, seafood restaurants, and souvenir shops.

These beaches showcase Sri Lanka's natural beauty and offer a variety of experiences, from relaxation to adventure, making them perfect for any beach lover or traveler seeking coastal bliss.

Enchanting Gardens in Sri Lanka

Sri Lanka is home to several enchanting gardens that showcase the country's lush greenery and diverse flora. Here are a few notable ones:

Royal Botanical Gardens, Peradeniya: Located near Kandy, these gardens are renowned for their extensive collection of orchids, exotic palms, and towering trees. Highlights include the Avenue of Royal Palms, the orchid house, and a giant Javan fig tree.

Hakgala Botanical Gardens: Situated near Nuwara Eliya, these gardens are known for their temperate climate and colorful blooms. The gardens feature a variety of roses, orchids, and an impressive collection of ferns.

Brief Garden, Bentota: Created by renowned Sri Lankan artist Bevis Bawa, this garden is a masterpiece of landscape design with winding pathways, hidden sculptures, and vibrant tropical plants. It offers a blend of natural beauty and artistic expression.

Lunuganga Estate: Another creation of Bevis Bawa, located near Bentota, this garden is a tranquil retreat with terraced gardens, water features, and serene views of the Dedduwa Lake.

It reflects Bawa's passion for blending architecture with nature.

Seethawaka Wet Zone Botanic Gardens: Located in Avissawella, these gardens focus on conserving Sri Lanka's wet zone flora. They feature a range of endemic plants, medicinal herbs, and educational exhibits on biodiversity conservation.

These gardens not only offer a peaceful escape but also provide insights into Sri Lanka's rich botanical heritage, making them delightful destinations for nature enthusiasts and travelers alike.

Sri Lanka Museums And Educational Attraction

Sri Lanka boasts several museums and educational attractions that offer insights into its history, culture, and natural heritage. Here are some notable ones:

National Museum of Colombo: Located in Colombo, this is the largest museum in Sri Lanka and houses a vast collection of artifacts, including ancient royal regalia, religious relics, and colonial-era exhibits. It provides a comprehensive overview of the island's cultural evolution.

Colombo Dutch Museum: Housed in a colonial-era Dutch building, this museum in Colombo showcases the Dutch colonial history in Sri Lanka. It features furniture, ceramics, and artifacts from the Dutch colonial period, offering a glimpse into their influence on the island.

Anuradhapura Archaeological Museum: Situated in the ancient city of Anuradhapura, this museum exhibits artifacts unearthed from the archaeological sites of Anuradhapura, providing insights into the ancient civilization and Buddhist heritage of Sri Lanka.

Galle Maritime Archaeological Museum: Located within Galle Fort, this museum highlights Sri Lanka's maritime history and showcases artifacts recovered from shipwrecks along the coast. It includes ceramics, coins, and navigational instruments from various historical periods.

Museum of Natural History, Colombo: Part of the National Museum complex, this museum focuses on Sri Lanka's natural heritage, displaying diverse flora, fauna, and geological specimens. It offers educational exhibits on the island's ecosystems and biodiversity.

Dambulla Cave Temple: Although not a traditional museum, this UNESCO World Heritage site in Dambulla houses a vast collection of Buddhist murals and statues within its cave complex. It serves as an educational attraction showcasing ancient Buddhist art and religious practices.

These museums and educational attractions provide visitors with a deeper understanding of Sri Lanka's cultural, historical, and natural diversity, making them enriching destinations for travelers interested in learning and exploration.

Zoos and Animal Encounters in Sri Lanka

Sri Lanka offers several opportunities for animal encounters and wildlife experiences. Here are some notable zoos and attractions:

Pinnawala Elephant Orphanage: Located near Kandy, Pinnawala is a sanctuary and orphanage for elephants. Visitors can observe elephants bathing in the river and learn about conservation efforts for these majestic animals.

Udawalawe National Park: While not a zoo, Udawalawe is a popular wildlife reserve where visitors can take safari tours to see elephants, leopards, deer, and a variety of bird species in their natural habitat.

Dehiwala Zoo: Situated in Colombo, the Dehiwala Zoo is Sri Lanka's oldest and largest zoo. It houses a diverse collection of animals, including elephants, lions, crocodiles, and exotic birds. The zoo also features educational exhibits on wildlife conservation.

Yala National Park: Known for its leopard population, Yala National Park is another renowned wildlife sanctuary in Sri Lanka. Safari tours offer the chance to spot leopards, elephants, sloth bears, and a wide array of birdlife amidst its diverse ecosystems.

Wilpattu National Park: Located in the northwest, Wilpattu is the largest national park in Sri Lanka and known for its dense forests and numerous lakes. It's a great place to see leopards, elephants, deer, and various bird species in a more rugged, less crowded setting.

These destinations provide opportunities for up-close encounters with Sri Lanka's wildlife and contribute to conservation efforts while offering memorable experiences for visitors interested in nature and animals.

Chapter 7: Transit Options And Costs For Getting Around In Sri Lanka

Getting around Sri Lanka offers several transit options, each varying in cost and convenience:

Sri Lanka Bus Service

Sri Lanka's bus service is a primary and affordable mode of transportation for both locals and tourists, offering extensive coverage across the island. Here are key points to note:

Types of Buses: Sri Lanka has a variety of buses, including government-operated (CTB - Ceylon Transport Board) and privately-owned buses. CTB buses are generally cheaper, with fares starting as low as LKR 30-50 ($0.15-$0.25 USD) for short distances. Private buses may offer more comfort and faster travel times on certain routes, with fares typically ranging from LKR 50-150 ($0.25-$0.75 USD) depending on the distance.

Routes: Buses connect almost every town and village in Sri Lanka, making them a convenient option for exploring both urban areas and remote regions. Major routes such as Colombo to Kandy or Colombo to Galle are well-serviced, providing easy access to popular tourist destinations.

Fares: Bus fares are affordable, with prices varying based on the distance traveled and the type of bus. Longer intercity routes can cost between LKR 100-400 ($0.50-$2 USD) or more for semi-luxury or luxury buses that offer air conditioning and more comfort.

Types of Services: Buses range from standard non-air-conditioned to semi-luxury and luxury options. Semi-luxury and luxury buses offer added comfort and amenities, but at a higher cost compared to regular buses.

Frequency: Buses generally operate on fixed schedules, with more frequent services on popular routes during peak hours. However, schedules can be less predictable in remote areas or during off-peak times.

Safety and Comfort: While buses are a cost-effective way to travel, especially for budget-conscious travelers, comfort levels can vary. It's advisable to choose reputable bus services and be mindful of personal belongings in crowded buses.

Overall, Sri Lanka's bus service provides an economical way to explore the country, offering insights into local life and culture while catering to different budget preferences.

Car rental in Sri Lanka

Renting a car in Sri Lanka is a convenient option for travelers looking to explore the island independently. Here's what you need to know about car rentals:

Rental Agencies: There are several international and local car rental agencies operating in Sri Lanka, especially in major cities like Colombo, Kandy, and Negombo. Popular international companies include Avis, Hertz, and Budget, while local agencies offer competitive rates and sometimes more flexible terms.

Booking: It's advisable to book your rental car in advance, especially during peak tourist seasons (December to April). Online platforms and travel agencies can provide options and allow you to compare prices and vehicle types.

Requirements: To rent a car in Sri Lanka, you typically need a valid driver's license from your home country or an International Driving Permit (IDP). Some rental companies may also require a minimum age (usually 21 or 25 years old) and a credit card for security deposit purposes.

Cost: Rental costs vary depending on the type of vehicle, rental duration, insurance coverage, and seasonality. On average, daily rental rates for a basic sedan or compact car range from $30 to $60 USD. Additional costs may include insurance (recommended for comprehensive coverage), GPS rental, and fuel expenses.

Driving: Sri Lanka follows left-hand traffic rules. Roads can vary from well-maintained highways to narrow, winding roads in rural areas. It's essential to drive defensively, especially in busy city traffic and on rural roads where livestock and pedestrians may be present.

Renting a car provides flexibility and convenience for exploring Sri Lanka's diverse landscapes and attractions at your own pace. Be sure to review rental agreements carefully and drive responsibly to enjoy a safe and memorable journey.

Train Services in Sri Lanka

Sure, here's the revised information including train costs in Sri Lanka:

Types of Trains:

 - *Intercity Express:* Fastest trains connecting major cities like Colombo, Kandy, and Galle. Air-conditioned options available.

- *Semi-Express:* Quicker than local trains, stopping at major and some intermediate stations.

- *Local Trains:* Budget-friendly option, stopping at most stations.

Popular Routes:

- Colombo to Kandy: Scenic route through hills and tea plantations.

- Colombo to Galle: Coastal journey offering views of beaches and villages.

- Colombo to Jaffna: Long-distance route to the northern part of the island.

Ticket Costs:

- Intercity Express: Prices vary; for example, Colombo to Kandy can range from LKR 400 (second class) to LKR 2,000 (first class).

- Semi-Express: Around LKR 250 to LKR 1,000 depending on distance and class.

- Local Trains: Very affordable, with prices starting from LKR 50 for shorter journeys.

Ticketing:

- Available at railway stations or online via Sri Lanka Railways website.

- First-class and second-class options with varying amenities.

Facilities:

- Some trains have dining cars or trolley services.

- Luggage storage available onboard or designated areas.

Tips for Travelers:

- Booking: Reserve tickets early, especially during peak seasons.

- Scenic Views: Opt for left-side seats when traveling Colombo to Kandy for better views.

- Comfort: Bring snacks and water for longer journeys.

Safety and Reliability:

- Generally safe; keep valuables secure.

- Check for schedule updates as delays can occur.

Local Experience:
- Enjoy the cultural experience and interact with locals during your journey.

These details should help you plan your train travel across Sri Lanka efficiently while considering costs and amenities.

Sri Lanka Ferry Transit System

Sure, here's the revised information including costs for ferry transit in Sri Lanka:

Overview:
- Ferry services in Sri Lanka provide convenient and scenic transportation between coastal cities and islands.
- They are popular among both locals and tourists for their accessibility and views.

Popular Routes:
- Colombo to Jaffna: Major route connecting the capital with the northern part of the island.
- Colombo to Trincomalee: Links the west coast to the eastern coast.

- Bentota to Galle: Shorter route along the southern coast.

Types of Ferries:
- **Passenger Ferries:** Basic services for passengers with limited luggage capacity.
- **Tourist Ferries:** More comfortable options with amenities such as seating areas and refreshments.

Ticket Costs:
- Prices range depending on the route and ferry type.
  - **For example:**
    - Colombo to Jaffna: Approximately LKR 1,000 to LKR 2,500.
    - Colombo to Trincomalee: Around LKR 800 to LKR 2,000.
    - Bentota to Galle: Approximately LKR 500 to LKR 1,000.

Ticketing:
- Tickets can be purchased at ferry terminals or through online platforms where available.

- It's recommended to book tickets in advance, especially during peak travel seasons.

Facilities:
- Basic amenities onboard, including seating and possibly refreshments on longer routes.
- Limited luggage storage; passengers should manage their belongings accordingly.

Tips for Travelers:
- **Schedule:** Check ferry schedules in advance as they may vary seasonally.
- **Comfort:** Be prepared for potential seasickness, especially on longer journeys.
- **Scenic Views:** Enjoy the coastal landscapes and ocean views during the ferry ride.

Safety and Reliability:
- Ferries maintain good safety standards, but passengers should follow crew instructions, especially during adverse weather conditions.
- Stay informed about weather updates that could affect ferry operations.

Local Experience:

- Embrace the unique experience of traveling by ferry in Sri Lanka, interacting with locals and enjoying the cultural aspects.

This detailed information should help you plan your ferry travels across Sri Lanka's coastal areas while considering costs and amenities available onboard.

Chapter 8: The "Must know" Guidelines For First-time Visitors To Sri Lanka

Sri Lanka Currency

Certainly! Here's a detailed comment on the currency of Sri Lanka:

Sri Lanka Currency Overview:
The official currency of Sri Lanka is the Sri Lankan Rupee (LKR), denoted by the symbol "Rs" or "Rs." One rupee is subdivided into 100 cents. Banknotes are available in denominations of 10, 20, 50, 100, 500, 1000, 2000, and 5000 rupees, while coins are issued in 1, 2, 5, and 10 rupee denominations.

Understanding the Sri Lankan currency ensures smooth financial transactions during your visit, whether exploring cultural sites, dining on local cuisine, or shopping for souvenirs.

Bring some Cash with you for Sri Lanka Tour

Here are the details on bringing cash for your tour in Sri Lanka:

Currency: The official currency of Sri Lanka is the Sri Lankan Rupee (LKR). It's advisable to carry rupees for convenience, especially in rural areas where card acceptance may be limited.

Currency Exchange: Exchange foreign currency for rupees upon arrival at airports, banks, or authorized exchange centers. ATMs are widely available in major cities and tourist areas for additional cash withdrawal.

Denominations: Banknotes come in denominations of 10, 20, 50, 100, 500, 1000, 2000, and 5000 rupees. Coins are available in 1, 2, 5, and 10 rupee denominations.

Where to Use Cash:

- **Local Markets:** Many local markets and smaller shops prefer cash transactions.

- **Transport:** Taxis, tuk-tuks, and buses often accept only cash payments.

- **Tips and Small Purchases:** Cash is handy for tipping, buying snacks, and paying for small services.

Safety Tips:

- **Exchange:** Use authorized money changers or banks to avoid counterfeit currency.

- **Security:** Keep cash secure and use money belts or hidden pouches for safety, especially in crowded areas.

Alternative Payment Methods:

- **Credit Cards:** Accepted in hotels, restaurants, and larger stores, but not universally in smaller establishments.

- **ATMs:** Accessible for withdrawals, but check fees and inform your bank of travel plans to avoid card issues.

Currency Value: Monitor exchange rates to maximize your budget and plan currency exchanges accordingly.

Bringing a mix of cash and alternative payment methods ensures you're prepared for various spending situations during your travels in Sri Lanka.

Where To Exchange Money in Sri Lanka

Here are three places where you can exchange money in Sri Lanka:

Airports: Currency exchange counters are available at Bandaranaike International Airport (Colombo Airport) and other major airports across the country. They offer convenient exchange services upon arrival.

Banks: Most banks in Sri Lanka provide currency exchange services. Visit bank branches in major cities like Colombo, Kandy, and Galle for competitive rates and secure transactions.

Authorized Money Changers: Authorized money changers or exchange bureaus are prevalent in tourist areas and cities. Look for reputable ones displaying authorized licenses to ensure reliable service and fair rates.

These options provide convenient access to exchange your currency for Sri Lankan Rupees (LKR) to facilitate your travel expenses throughout the country.

Health Tips for Sri Lanka Tourists

Here are essential health tips for tourists visiting Sri Lanka:

Vaccinations: Ensure routine vaccinations are up to date. Consider vaccinations for hepatitis A, typhoid, and tetanus. Malaria prophylaxis may be recommended for certain regions.

Water and Food Safety: Drink bottled or boiled water and avoid ice in drinks. Eat freshly cooked and hot foods. Be cautious with raw vegetables and fruits that may have been washed in local water.

Insect Protection: Use insect repellent containing DEET and wear long-sleeved clothing and pants, especially during dusk and dawn, to prevent mosquito bites. Consider mosquito nets if accommodations are not adequately screened.

Sun Protection: Sri Lanka's tropical climate means strong sun exposure. Use sunscreen with a high SPF, wear a hat and sunglasses, and seek shade during peak sun hours.

Medical Insurance: Obtain comprehensive travel medical insurance that covers medical expenses, including evacuation if necessary. Check if your insurance covers adventure activities like surfing or hiking.

Healthcare Facilities: While major cities have hospitals and clinics with modern facilities, remote areas may have limited medical services. Carry a basic medical kit with essentials like bandages, pain relievers, and any personal medications.

Dengue Fever Awareness: Dengue fever is endemic in Sri Lanka. Protect against mosquito bites and seek medical attention if you experience symptoms such as high fever, severe headache, and joint pain.

Hygiene Practices: Maintain good hygiene, including regular handwashing, to prevent gastrointestinal illnesses and other infections.

By following these health tips, you can enjoy a safe and healthy trip to Sri Lanka while exploring its diverse landscapes and cultural attractions.

Sri Lanka Emergency Contacts

Here are important emergency contacts for travelers in Sri Lanka:

Police: Dial *119* for emergency police assistance.

Ambulance / Medical Emergency: Dial *1990* for ambulance services.

Fire Department: Dial *110* for fire emergencies.

Tourist Police: Dial *1912* for assistance related to tourist safety and support.

These contacts are essential for quick assistance in case of emergencies while traveling in Sri Lanka. It's advisable to save these numbers and keep them accessible during your stay.

Sri Lanka Cultural Étiquettes

Understanding cultural etiquette in Sri Lanka is essential for respectful and enjoyable interactions:

Greetings: Use a slight bow or a gentle handshake when greeting someone. The traditional greeting "Ayubowan" (may you have a long life) is appreciated.

Respect for Religious Sites: Remove shoes and hats before entering temples and religious sites. Dress modestly with shoulders and knees covered.

Public Behavior: Public displays of affection are uncommon and best avoided. Respect local customs and traditions.

Gift Giving: When invited to a Sri Lankan home, bring a small gift like sweets or fruits. Gifts are usually given and received with both hands.

Eating Etiquette: Eat with your right hand, especially when dining with locals. It's polite to try local dishes and accept food offerings graciously.

Photography: Ask for permission before photographing people, especially at religious ceremonies or in rural areas. Respect signs prohibiting photography in certain locations.

Tipping: Tipping is customary, especially in hotels and restaurants where a 10% service charge may not be included. A small tip for services like taxi rides is appreciated.

Environmental Respect: Avoid littering and respect wildlife and natural habitats, particularly in national parks and eco-sensitive areas.

Adhering to these cultural etiquettes fosters positive interactions and demonstrates respect for Sri Lanka's rich cultural heritage.

Chapter 9: Financial Planning and Budgeting for Sri Lanka tour

Plan your Sri Lanka tour budget wisely: account for transport, accommodations, food, activities, and unexpected costs to ensure a memorable and stress-free experience.

The Need For Financial Planning As A Tourist in Sri Lanka

Financial planning is crucial for tourists visiting Sri Lanka to ensure a smooth and enjoyable trip. Here are five reasons why it's essential:

Budget Allocation:

- *Accommodations:* Determine your lodging preferences and allocate funds accordingly, whether for budget hostels, mid-range hotels, or luxury resorts.

- *Transportation:* Budget for taxis, tuk-tuks, or private drivers depending on your travel preferences and distances between destinations.

- *Activities:* Plan for entrance fees to attractions, guided tours, cultural experiences, and adventure activities like safaris or water sports.

- *Food and Dining:* Include daily meals, snacks, and dining out experiences, considering both local eateries and higher-end restaurants.

- *Incidentals:* Set aside funds for unforeseen expenses like medical emergencies, souvenirs, tips, and additional costs not initially budgeted.

Currency Exchange and Payments:

- Research the exchange rate between your home currency and Sri Lankan Rupees (LKR) to estimate daily spending.

- Ensure you have a mix of payment options such as cash (for small purchases and markets) and credit/debit cards (for larger expenses and emergencies).

- Keep in mind that some places may not accept cards, so having cash on hand is advisable, especially in rural areas.

Avoiding Overspending:

- Establish a daily spending limit to stay within your overall budget.

- Track expenses using apps or spreadsheets to monitor spending patterns and adjust accordingly.

- Be mindful of tourist traps and inflated prices in high-traffic areas; negotiate prices when possible, especially in markets and with local vendors.

Emergency Preparedness:

- Carry a backup source of funds, such as traveler's checks or a separate credit card, in case of loss or theft.

- Research emergency services and contact numbers, including your embassy or consulate, for assistance with financial issues or emergencies.

- Plan for unexpected costs, such as unplanned medical expenses or flight changes, by having a contingency fund.

Maximizing Experience:

- By planning your finances effectively, you can prioritize experiences that matter most to you, whether it's cultural immersion, outdoor adventures, or relaxation.

- Budgeting allows you to make informed decisions about where to splurge and where to save, ensuring you get the most out of your Sri Lanka tour without financial stress.

Financial planning as a tourist in Sri Lanka ensures you have the resources to enjoy your trip to the fullest while maintaining financial stability and preparedness for any unforeseen circumstances.

Money Saving For First Time Tourists to Sri Lanka

Saving money as a first-time tourist in Sri Lanka involves smart planning and budget-conscious decisions. Here are practical tips to help you save:

Travel Off-Peak:
- Visit during shoulder seasons (April-May and September-November) to find lower accommodation rates and fewer crowds.

Accommodation Choices:
- Opt for guesthouses, homestays, or budget hotels instead of luxury resorts. Consider booking directly or through local platforms for better deals.

Local Transport:
- Use public buses and trains, which are inexpensive and provide an authentic Sri Lankan travel experience. Tuk-tuks (three-wheeler taxis) are cheaper for short distances compared to private taxis.

Eating Local:
- Enjoy Sri Lankan street food and local eateries where meals are affordable and flavorful. Look for "rice and curry" spots for filling and budget-friendly meals.

Free Attractions and Activities:
- Explore temples, parks, and beaches that don't charge entrance fees. Take advantage of

cultural festivals and events for enriching experiences at no cost.

Currency Exchange and Fees:

- Minimize currency exchange fees by withdrawing large amounts at ATMs and using credit cards with no foreign transaction fees where possible.

By implementing these money-saving strategies, you can stretch your budget further and make the most of your first-time visit to Sri Lanka without compromising on experiences or comfort.

Tips for Bargaining and Negotiating in Sri Lanka

Bargaining and negotiating in Sri Lanka can be a cultural experience in itself. Here are five tips to help you navigate this practice effectively:

Start with a Smile and Politeness:

- Approach bargaining with a friendly demeanor. Start negotiations with a smile and polite greetings. Building rapport can lead to better deals.

Know the Market Price:
- Research beforehand to understand the general price range for the item or service you're interested in. This knowledge helps you set a reasonable starting point for negotiations.

Practice Patience:
- Bargaining in Sri Lanka is often a slower process compared to Western cultures. Remain patient and avoid showing frustration or impatience, as this can hinder successful negotiations.

Offer a Counter Price:
- After the initial price is quoted, counter with a lower offer that reflects your researched market price. Expect some back-and-forth negotiation until you reach a mutually acceptable price.

By approaching bargaining with respect for local customs and a willingness to engage in friendly negotiation, you can often secure better prices while enjoying a cultural exchange with sellers in Sri Lanka.

Tips To help Avoid Crowds While Shopping/ Touring Sri Lanka

Avoiding crowds while shopping and touring in Sri Lanka can enhance your experience. Here are five tips to help you achieve this:

Visit Early or Late:

- Plan your visits to popular attractions, markets, and tourist spots early in the morning or later in the afternoon. This avoids peak hours when crowds are largest.

Explore Off-the-Beaten-Path Locations:

- Venture beyond the main tourist areas to discover quieter, lesser-known spots. This can include local markets, neighborhoods, or scenic spots off the typical tourist route.

Choose Non-Peak Seasons:
- Travel during shoulder seasons or off-peak months (outside major holidays and festivals) to encounter fewer tourists and enjoy more peaceful surroundings.

Use Local Insight:
- Seek advice from locals or your accommodations for recommendations on less crowded times to visit popular attractions or markets. They can provide valuable insights based on local knowledge.

Plan Your Itinerary Wisely:
- Spread out your itinerary to include visits to popular sites on weekdays rather than weekends. This can significantly reduce crowds as local visitors often frequent attractions on weekends.

By implementing these tips, you can navigate Sri Lanka with fewer crowds, allowing for more relaxed and enjoyable experiences during your travels.

Chapter 10: Sri Lanka Day Trips & Excursions

Sri Lanka's day trips and excursions offer a kaleidoscope of experiences, from exploring ancient temples and lush tea plantations to relaxing on pristine beaches and encountering diverse wildlife. Each journey unveils a tapestry of culture, nature, and adventure, making every day trip an enriching adventure in this tropical paradise.

Nature and Wildlife in Sri Lanka

Sri Lanka boasts rich biodiversity and stunning landscapes, making it a haven for nature and wildlife enthusiasts. Here's an in-depth look at the nature and wildlife of Sri Lanka:

Biodiversity and Habitats:

- *Flora:* Sri Lanka is home to diverse ecosystems ranging from tropical rainforests to dry plains and highland forests. It hosts over 3,000 flowering plant species, including endemic orchids and medicinal plants.

- *Fauna:* The island is renowned for its wildlife diversity, with over 120 species of mammals, including elephants, leopards, sloth bears, and primates like langurs and macaques. Sri Lanka is also famous for its birdlife, with around 433 recorded species, including endemic species like the Sri Lanka junglefowl and Sri Lanka blue magpie.

National Parks and Reserves:

- *Yala National Park:* Located in the southeast, Yala is known for its dense leopard population, along with elephants, sloth bears, and a variety of bird species.

- *Wilpattu National Park:* Sri Lanka's largest national park, famous for its natural lakes (villus) and the chance to spot leopards, elephants, and sloth bears.

- *Minneriya National Park:* Known for the annual gathering of elephants during the dry season ("The Gathering"), where hundreds of elephants congregate around the Minneriya Tank.

Marine Life:

- Sri Lanka's coastal waters are rich in marine biodiversity, with vibrant coral reefs and over 30 species of whales and dolphins found offshore. Mirissa and Trincomalee are popular for whale watching tours.

Conservation Efforts:

- Sri Lanka has several conservation initiatives aimed at preserving its natural heritage. Efforts include protecting endangered species, reforestation projects, and sustainable tourism practices in national parks and reserves.

Ecotourism Opportunities:

- Visitors can engage in a range of ecotourism activities such as guided safaris, birdwatching tours, trekking through rainforests, and camping in designated areas. These activities promote conservation awareness and support local communities.

Cultural Significance:

- Wildlife and nature hold cultural significance in Sri Lanka, reflected in ancient myths, art, and religious beliefs. Sacred sites like Ritigala are nestled within natural landscapes, blending spirituality with biodiversity conservation.

Sri Lanka's remarkable biodiversity and natural beauty make it a captivating destination for nature lovers and wildlife enthusiasts alike. Whether exploring its lush jungles, encountering majestic elephants, or witnessing marine marvels, the island offers unforgettable experiences immersed in its natural wonders.

Sri Lanka Solo Travel

Solo travel in Sri Lanka offers a unique and rewarding experience for adventurous travelers. Here's a detailed overview:

Safety and Security:

- Sri Lanka is generally safe for solo travelers, with a low crime rate. Exercise usual precautions, especially in crowded areas and at night. Stay informed about local news and travel advisories.

Transportation:

- Getting around Sri Lanka solo is manageable. Opt for reliable modes like trains and buses for long-distance travel between cities and regions. Tuk-tuks are convenient for short distances within towns and cities.

Accommodation:

- Accommodation options range from budget hostels and guesthouses to mid-range hotels and boutique stays. Book accommodations in advance, especially during peak seasons, to secure preferred choices.

Cultural Exploration:

- Embrace Sri Lanka's rich culture and heritage by exploring ancient temples, historical sites like Anuradhapura and Polonnaruwa, and vibrant markets. Engage with locals to learn about their traditions and lifestyles.

Adventure and Nature:

- Sri Lanka offers diverse outdoor activities for solo travelers, including trekking in the central highlands (e.g., Ella Rock), wildlife safaris in national parks (e.g., Yala), surfing in Arugam Bay, and hiking to waterfalls like Diyaluma.

Solo travel in Sri Lanka offers independence, cultural immersion, and opportunities for exploration across its scenic landscapes and diverse attractions. With careful planning and awareness, solo travelers can enjoy a memorable and enriching experience in this island paradise.

Safety Tips for Sri Lanka Solo travelers

Solo travelers in Sri Lanka can enhance their safety with these essential tips:

Stay Informed: Stay updated on local news and travel advisories before and during your trip. Be aware of any safety concerns or political developments that may affect your travel plans.

Choose Safe Accommodations: Opt for reputable hotels, guesthouses, or hostels with positive reviews and secure facilities. Research accommodations in advance and book trusted options.

Secure Transportation: Use licensed taxis, rideshare services, or trusted tuk-tuk drivers for transportation. Avoid traveling alone late at night, especially in unfamiliar or secluded areas.

Keep Valuables Secure: Keep your belongings, including passports, cash, and electronics, secure at all times. Use a money belt or secure bag to carry essentials when exploring.

Share Your Itinerary: Inform a trusted person about your travel plans, including accommodations and activities. Stay in touch regularly and share updates on your whereabouts.

By following these safety tips, solo travelers can enjoy a rewarding and secure experience exploring the beauty and culture of Sri Lanka.

7-Day Sri Lanka Travel Plan

Here's a suggested 7-day travel plan for Sri Lanka, highlighting key activities and destinations:

Day 1: Arrival in Colombo
- Arrive in Colombo, Sri Lanka's capital.
- Explore Colombo city sights like Gangaramaya Temple and Independence Square.
- Visit local markets for shopping and dining experiences.

Day 2: Sigiriya and Dambulla
- Travel to Sigiriya and climb Sigiriya Rock Fortress, a UNESCO World Heritage site.
- Visit Dambulla Cave Temple, renowned for its ancient Buddhist murals and statues.
- Overnight stay in Sigiriya or Dambulla.

Day 3: Kandy

- Head to Kandy, visiting the Sacred Temple of the Tooth Relic.
- Explore the Peradeniya Botanical Gardens, featuring a variety of plant species.
- Attend a cultural dance performance in the evening.

Day 4: Nuwara Eliya
- Travel to Nuwara Eliya, known for its tea plantations and cool climate.
- Visit a tea estate and learn about tea production processes.
- Explore Gregory Lake and surrounding parks.
- Overnight stay in Nuwara Eliya.

Day 5: Ella
- Take a scenic train ride from Nuwara Eliya to Ella, passing through picturesque landscapes.
- Hike to Ella Rock for panoramic views of the hill country.
- Visit Nine Arches Bridge, an iconic railway bridge surrounded by lush greenery.

Day 6: Yala National Park

- Travel to Yala National Park for a morning safari, known for its diverse wildlife including leopards, elephants, and birds.
- Enjoy wildlife spotting and explore the park's natural beauty.
- Overnight stay near Yala National Park.

Day 7: Mirissa

- Head to Mirissa for whale watching or a relaxing beach day.
- Optionally visit Galle Fort, a UNESCO World Heritage site known for its colonial architecture.
- Departure from Colombo or extension of stay as per your travel plans.

This itinerary offers a mix of cultural exploration, natural beauty, and wildlife experiences across Sri Lanka's diverse landscapes, catering to various interests and preferences. Adjustments can be made based on personal preferences and seasonal considerations.

Helpful websites and Resources for Tourists in Sri Lanka

For tourists planning a trip to Sri Lanka, here are some helpful websites and resources:

Tourism Sri Lanka Official Website: Provides official information on attractions, accommodations, festivals, and travel tips. [Tourism Sri Lanka](http://www.srilanka.travel/)

Visit Sri Lanka by Tourism Development Authority: Official tourism site featuring travel guides, itineraries, and practical information. [Visit Sri Lanka](https://www.visitsrilanka.com/)

Expat.com Sri Lanka Forum: Discussions and tips from expatriates and locals about living and traveling in Sri Lanka. [Expat.com Sri Lanka Forum](https://www.expat.com/forum/viewforum.php?id=830)

Travel Blogs: Blogs like Nomadic Matt, The Culture Trip, and Sri Lanka Travel Blogs offer personal insights, tips, and detailed travel experiences.

Weather and Climate Information: Check weather forecasts and climate details at [Weather.com](https://weather.com/) or [AccuWeather](https://www.accuweather.com/) to plan your trip effectively.

These resources provide valuable information and tools to enhance your travel planning and ensure a memorable experience in Sri Lanka.

Tourists friendly Apps

For tourists visiting Sri Lanka, here are some useful and tourist-friendly apps to consider:

PickMe: A popular ridesharing app in Sri Lanka similar to Uber, offering convenient and reliable transportation options including tuk-tuks.

Google Maps: Essential for navigating cities, finding attractions, and planning routes for both walking and driving.

YAMU: A local app featuring reviews and recommendations for restaurants, cafes, and attractions across Sri Lanka.

XE Currency: Useful for converting currencies and keeping track of exchange rates while traveling.

These apps can enhance your travel experience in Sri Lanka by providing navigation, recommendations, transportation options, and essential information at your fingertips.

Conclusion

Planning a trip to Sri Lanka involves exploring its rich cultural heritage, diverse landscapes, and vibrant wildlife. Whether you're drawn to ancient temples, lush tea plantations, or thrilling safaris, Sri Lanka offers a mosaic of experiences.

Printed in Great Britain
by Amazon